Social Media

Connect with a community of *Bible Studies for Life* users. Post responses to questions, share teaching ideas, and link to great blog content. **Facebook.com/BibleStudiesForLife**

Get instant updates about new articles, giveaways, and more. **@BibleMeetsLife**

The App

Simple and straightforward, this elegantly designed iPhone app gives you all the content of the Small Group Member Book—plus a whole lot more—right at your fingertips. Available in the iTunes App Store; search **"Bible Studies for Life."**

Blog

At **BibleStudiesForLife.com/blog** you will find magazine articles and music downloads from LifeWay Worship. Plus, leaders and group members alike will benefit from the blog posts written for people in every life stage—singles, parents, boomers, and senior adults—as well as media clips, connections between our study topics, current events, and much more.

Let Hope In
Bible Studies for Life: Small Group Member Book

© 2013 LifeWay Press®

ISBN: 978-1-4300-2898-7

Item: 005602634

Dewey Decimal Classification Number: 234

Subject Heading: HOPE \ DISAPPOINTMENT \ CHRISTIAN LIFE

Eric Geiger
Vice President, Church Resources

Ronnie Floyd
General Editor

David Francis
Managing Editor

Gena Rogers
Karen Dockrey
Content Editors

Philip Nation
Director, Adult Ministry Publishing

Faith Whatley
Director, Adult Ministry

Send questions/comments to: Content Editor, *Bible Studies for Life: Adults*, One LifeWay Plaza, Nashville, TN 37234-0175; or make comments on the Web at *www.BibleStudiesforLife.com*.

Printed in the United States of America

For ordering or inquiries, visit *www.lifeway.com*; write LifeWay Small Groups; One LifeWay Plaza; Nashville, TN 37234-0152; or call toll free (800) 458-2772.

W9-AHB-416

Hope changes *everything*

We all need hope. Maybe we've made mistakes. Maybe we feel shame or regret over something in our present or past. We've tried to fix things in our lives and we've failed. If we're not careful we can be blinded by an onslaught of mistakes, shame, and regret. And in this blindness we can lose sight of hope.

The Bible tells us that hope helps us through periods of blindness because the love of God has been poured out within our hearts through the Holy Spirit. The Bible also tells us that we can rejoice when we run into trials because they help us endure. This endurance gives us strength which gives us character which gives us … hope.

Even those among us who seem to have it all together have areas of hurt in our lives. This study will show you the way to hope regardless of your past. You no longer have to be bound or hindered by regrets and shame. You can know and experience hope. And that hope can transform you daily.

Pete Wilson

Let Hope In is a small-group study by Pete Wilson, who authored the book *Let Hope In: 4 Choices That Will Change Your Life Forever* (Thomas Nelson, 2013).

Pete is the founding and senior pastor of Cross Point Church in Nashville, Tennessee, a committed church community that he and his wife, Brandi, planted in 2002. Cross Point has grown to reach more than 5,000 people each weekend through its five campuses located around the Nashville area and online. Follow Pete on Twitter: @pwilson or read his blog at *WithoutWax.tv*.

contents

SESSION 1

HOPE NEEDED

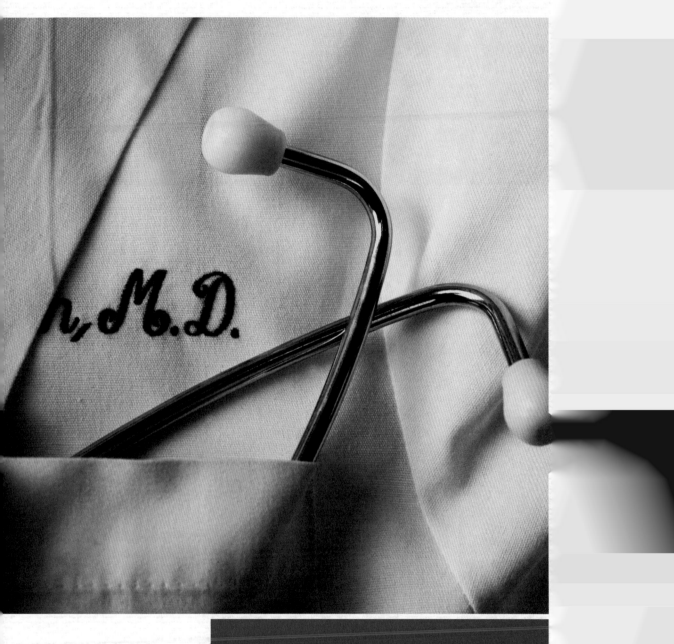

What did you want to be when you grew up?

You are never beyond hope.

THE BIBLE MEETS LIFE

Veterinarians, astronauts, doctors, presidents, and maybe even a superhero or two. These are the future occupations of third graders everywhere. Why? Children have their entire lives ahead of them. At their age the sky is the limit, there's time to dream, and it's always OK to hope for a better tomorrow.

What if your entire life were ahead of you, too? What if your tomorrow could be better than your yesterday? That's what hope is about, being free from your past to create a new future. We look forward to the life ahead of us when we're young. Yet with each passing year, mistakes enter the picture. Bad decisions. Sin. Our past begins to overtake our future and we lose hope. Hope becomes a concept for other people: *It's too late for me.*

We all need hope. That is universal. But there is an even greater universal truth: hope is possible. Hope is reality. In this Bible study we consider the life of one man who saw himself beyond hope but found the opposite to be true.

WHAT DOES THE BIBLE SAY?

2 Samuel 9:6-13 (HCSB)

6 Mephibosheth son of Jonathan son of Saul came to David, bowed down to the ground and paid homage. David said, "Mephibosheth!" "I am your servant," he replied.

7 "Don't be afraid," David said to him, "since I intend to show you kindness because of your father Jonathan. I will restore to you all your grandfather Saul's fields, and you will always eat meals at my table."

8 Mephibosheth bowed down and said, "What is your servant that you take an interest in a dead dog like me?"

9 Then the king summoned Saul's attendant Ziba and said to him, "I have given to your master's grandson all that belonged to Saul and his family.

10 You, your sons, and your servants are to work the ground for him, and you are to bring in the crops so your master's grandson will have food to eat. But Mephibosheth, your master's grandson, is always to eat at my table." Now Ziba had 15 sons and 20 servants.

11 Ziba said to the king, "Your servant will do all my lord the king commands." So Mephibosheth ate at David's table just like one of the king's sons.

12 Mephibosheth had a young son whose name was Mica. All those living in Ziba's house were Mephibosheth's servants.

13 However, Mephibosheth lived in Jerusalem because he always ate at the king's table. His feet had been injured.

Key Words

paid homage (v. 6)—This phrase described how an individual would prostrate himself before a distinguished person in the sense of paying respect or reverence.

dead dog (v. 8)—Calling someone a dog signified absolute contempt. It was parallel to calling someone a mongrel or a scoundrel, comparable to cursing someone. Calling someone a dead dog doubled the insult.

2 Samuel 9:6-7

If ever a person had a right to give up on hope, it was Mephibosheth. He was the grandson of the former King Saul, who had tried to kill David and thwart his ascent to the throne. Saul had been David's most powerful enemy. So Mephibosheth was the grandson of David's worst enemy. That's the kind of family heritage you don't want while David is king.

But it gets worse.

First, Mephibosheth couldn't walk. When his grandfather, King Saul, died, his family feared for their lives. They made a hasty escape from what they thought would be the coming wrath of David. It was common in that culture for kings to kill the entire families of their enemies. During their escape, a nanny dropped the young Mephibosheth and his feet were crippled (see 2 Sam. 4:4). It was an accident. And, as the saying goes, accidents happen. Yet we still suffer from them.

Second, Mephibosheth suffered exile as a consequence of having King Saul as his grandfather. Saul chose to be David's enemy. This was something outside of Mephibosheth's control. Saul had made the choice, even before Mephibosheth was born. Mephibosheth inherited suffering from the choices of other people.

Mephibosheth was living in Lo-debar, which can mean "no communication," "no word," or "no pasture." No one forced him to live where he was. He made a choice—perhaps out of fear or shame. Exile may have come from the choices of others, but the choice to live in such an isolated place was his own choice.

We all, in our own way, are like Mephibosheth.

▶ **1.** We have experienced suffering that was no one's fault, but was due to circumstances.

▶ **2.** We have experienced suffering that was directly due to the sinful actions of others.

▶ **3.** We have experienced suffering that was due to our own poor choices.

> *What was a circumstance that caused you to feel hopeless?*

QUESTION #2

LOOKING BACK

How has one of the following tempted you to feel hopeless?

Circumstances

Someone else's choices

My own choices

2 Samuel 9:8

David reached out to Mephibosheth, but Mephibosheth didn't know the nature of David's inquiry. For all he knew, David was coming to kill him. I wonder what Mephibosheth was thinking when he approached David. He bowed down and referred to himself as a "dead dog." He saw himself as unworthy of hope, unworthy of any offering of grace. This pathetic phrase reveals so much about how Mephibosheth saw himself, how his identity had been shaped and solidified by tragedy and pain.

▶ The years of being ostracized

▶ The years of disability

▶ The years of wondering if God had cursed him or hated him

In Mephibosheth's journey, two things kept his hopelessness alive and well: shame and regret.

▶ Guilt says, "I did something wrong" while shame says, "I am wrong." Shame deceptively leads me to believe that I deserve to be shackled to it the rest of my life.

▶ Regret is what I feel when I've done something I wish I hadn't. When regret is not dealt with directly and redemptively, it leads to more regret.

Shame and regret both have the ability to keep me from seeing the hope right in front of me.

Mephibosheth struggled to see himself as David saw him. He struggled to understand that the goodness of the king was more powerful than the suffering of his past. Mephibosheth could stay trapped by shame and regret … or he could embrace the hope in front of him. He was not beyond hope.

> *Why is it difficult for people to let go of the past and move forward?*

QUESTION #3

"Trust the past to the mercy of God, the present to His love, and the future to His providence."

—AUGUSTINE OF HIPPO

When has God blessed you in an unexpected way?

QUESTION #4

2 Samuel 9:9-13

Mephibosheth was probably hoping his death would be quick and painless. Then he heard David speak these words: "Don't be afraid" (v. 7). How have you responded to the good gifts God has given you?

- ▶ **Insecurity:** Do I really deserve this?
- ▶ **Skepticism:** What's the catch?
- ▶ **Excitement:** This is so great!
- ▶ **Guilt:** I shouldn't accept this.

Mephibosheth initially may have questioned why David would offer him such hope. Even so, he wisely chose to embrace and live the hope. The king treated Mephibosheth and his son as if they were his own family. Mephibosheth lived out the rest of his days in Jerusalem, eating at the king's table.

Mephibosheth experienced the fulfillment of hope in three different ways:

1. The choices of others no longer were held against him.

2. He was set free from his own poor choices.

3. The king restored him.

This is what God does in our lives. He doesn't hold the choices of others against us. He forgives us for our past. He gives us good gifts we often never see coming.

How does embracing hope change you and others?

QUESTION #5

LIVE IT OUT

Mephibosheth suffered due to circumstances, sinful actions of others, and his own poor choices. But still he chose to embrace hope.

▶ **Appreciate a kindness.** Look around. How is God imparting hope to you through another person?

▶ **Forgive yourself.** What hurtful actions have you chosen that have brought you guilt and shame? Repent (turn from old ways), receive God's forgiveness, and start living with His hope.

▶ **Be an agent of hope to someone trapped by his or her past.** Offer friendship and encouragement— minus any judgment. Unsure of what to say or do? Share the gospel. Imitate Christ's unconditional love in your speech and behavior.

The past may offer shame and regret, but you can let God's hope shape your future. **Your entire life is ahead of you.**

Shadow of a Doubt

I remember waking one night, only a few months after accepting Jesus as Lord, in sheer terror that somehow my salvation wasn't real. Maybe I had said the wrong thing or God didn't hear me.

To continue reading "Shadow of a Doubt" from *HomeLife* magazine, visit *BibleStudiesforLife.com/articles*.

My group's prayer requests

....

....

....

....

....

....

....

....

....

My thoughts

SESSION 2

HOPE FOUND

When have you lost something important to you?

QUESTION *#1*

#BSFLfound

When we seek Christ, we find hope.

THE BIBLE MEETS LIFE

Your stomach drops. Your heart races. You realize you've lost something important. Whether it's a credit card, a wallet, a phone, or a purse, we've all experienced that feeling and it is one of the worst in the world.

Then comes the search, as you look in all the usual spots: the car, your room, couch cushions, everywhere. You retrace your steps. You consider calling on a search party.

And then comes that rush of relief: the server held on to your credit card; you find your purse in your car; or you discover your wallet wedged between the cushions on the couch. All the fears and worst-case scenarios melt away. Your heart resumes its normal rate again.

Look long enough and most personal items can be found. But what about something abstract like hope? Can one ever truly *find* it? In Matthew 8 we see Jesus interact with a leper and a Roman centurion. More importantly we find an answer.

WHAT DOES THE BIBLE SAY?

Matthew 8:1-13 *(HCSB)*

1 When He came down from the mountain, large crowds followed Him. 2 Right away a man with a serious skin disease came up and knelt before Him, saying, "Lord, if You are willing, You can make me clean." 3 Reaching out His hand He touched him, saying, "I am willing; be made clean." Immediately his disease was healed. 4 Then Jesus told him, "See that you don't tell anyone; but go, show yourself to the priest, and offer the gift that Moses prescribed, as a testimony to them."

5 When He entered Capernaum, a centurion came to Him, pleading with Him, 6 "Lord, my servant is lying at home paralyzed, in terrible agony!" 7 "I will come and heal him," He told him. 8 "Lord," the centurion replied, "I am not worthy to have You come under my roof. But only say the word, and my servant will be cured. 9 For I too am a man under authority, having soldiers under my command. I say to this one, 'Go!' and he goes; and to another, 'Come!' and he comes; and to my slave, 'Do this!' and he does it."

10 Hearing this, Jesus was amazed and said to those following Him, "I assure you: I have not found anyone in Israel with so great a faith! 11 I tell you that many will come from east and west, and recline at the table with Abraham, Isaac, and Jacob in the kingdom of heaven. 12 But the sons of the kingdom will be thrown into the outer darkness. In that place there will be weeping and gnashing of teeth." 13 Then Jesus told the centurion, "Go. As you have believed, let it be done for you." And his servant was cured that very moment.

Key Words

serious skin disease (v. 2)— Literally, "a leprous man." Leprosy's symptoms ranged from scaly white skin to oozing sores to the loss of fingers, toes, or other body parts.

centurion (v. 5)—This term referred to a Roman army officer who commanded around one hundred soldiers.

outer darkness (v. 12)— Some Jewish texts used this term to describe hell, where the wicked will be shut out from the light of heaven.

Matthew 8:1-4

In Matthew's account of Jesus' life we see Jesus interact with people in surprising ways. The first encounter in chapter 8 is with a man with a serious skin disease known as leprosy. In Bible times, the term *leprosy* was used for a variety of skin disorders from psoriasis to leprosy. Today leprosy is commonly called Hansen's disease. In this disease, slow-growing bacteria damage the nerves. It takes away the ability to sense pain. This loss of feeling can allow people to harm themselves without realizing it.

Leprosy is contagious; but you can only catch it if you come into close and repeated contact with moisture from the infected person's nose and mouth. Because of its contagious nature, people with leprosy were banished from their homes and cast beyond the protection of the city walls. Lepers lived isolated lives; they had to shout "unclean" anytime someone healthy came near. And lepers certainly were not allowed to approach anyone—especially not rabbis.

Yet that is exactly what this leper did. He knelt before Jesus to make the boldest request a man in his situation could make. "Lord, if you are willing, You can make me clean."

I imagine there was a pause. All the people must have stopped dead in their tracks. Then panicked shrieks and the noise of shuffling feet may have taken over as the people scrambled to get away from this man with the horrific disease. I imagine the man looking up to see if Jesus was one of those running away.

Yet Jesus stood there. With compassion in His eyes and an outstretched hand, this Rabbi did the unthinkable. He touched the untouchable. And He said, "I am willing; be made clean."

Leprosy = toxic people in life

> *How might sin in our lives make us feel like a leper?*
>
> QUESTION #2

> *Why might someone think Jesus would be unwilling to help?*
>
> QUESTION #3

Matthew 8:5-9

Ever tried to contest a phone bill? If you ask for a refund, credit, or discount, you might hear something like, "I'm sorry, but I'm not allowed to do that." Try asking the person taking your tickets at the game to stop the rain. Or ask the drivers next to you on the highway to make the traffic go away.

There are some things in life we have no power or authority over. The reality is that there are some things only God can do. There are some things only God can forgive, some grace only God can extend, some acceptance only God can provide, and some problems only God can fix. Yet often times we try to do it ourselves.

Jesus encountered another man in Matthew 8. This man was quite different from the leper; he was a centurion with the Roman military. A typical centurion had about one hundred men under his command. So this centurion knew how to be in charge. He knew how to lead others. He knew how to get things done. But when his servant became sick, the centurion could do nothing about it.

We don't know what the centurion tried on his own. Whatever the details, coming to Jesus would have been a hard step: Not only would this centurion have been considered an unclean Gentile, but he was despised all the more because his job was a reminder to the Jewish people they had been conquered. Having been stationed in the area, the centurion had surely experienced the disdain of the Jews. Orthodox Jews hated the Romans.

Would this one Jewish rabbi exhibit the same attitude? The centurion swallowed any pride and acknowledged his unworthiness in the eyes of the rabbi. He submissively called Jesus "Lord." The unspoken question underneath the centurion's request for healing reflected the words of the leper: would Jesus be willing?

* you will hold the stars

> **Since Jesus' authority is our only hope, why do we look for hope in other things or people?**

QUESTION #4

WHAT HOPE LOOKS LIKE

How is this like hope in Christ? How is it different from hope in Christ?

"There are two very different types of hope in this world. One is hoping for something and the other is hoping in someone."

—PETE WILSON

In your daily life, what is the evidence that you have hope in Christ?

QUESTION #5

Matthew 8:10-13

Jesus praised the centurion's faith. Jesus pronounced the servant would be cured. The servant was cured at that very moment. When the centurion got home, he found his servant healthy, healed, and alive.

Faith is trust. Jesus praised the centurion for his faith. He showed faith through his willingness to trust Jesus. He trusted that Jesus could heal his servant right there on the spot without ever venturing into the servant's presence.

Jesus doesn't simply want us to trust in Him or to find our hope in Him for certain things. He wants us to find hope in Him for all things. He wants us to trust in Him for everything.

The centurion's journey to faith culminated in finally asking Jesus for help, yet asking for help can be the hardest thing to do. "Jesus, help me" is one of the most honorable things we could ever say. The person who has what he thinks he needs doesn't ask for help. The spiritually destitute person has nothing to offer … and that is exactly what God requires of us.

Trusting Jesus is allowing Him to do for us what we cannot do for ourselves. When we learn to lean on Christ, we open the door to let hope in. We are not exempt from trouble. We are not exempt from hurt and brokenness, but we can have a confidence that Jesus has overcome the world and our past. There is hope in surrendering to Him.

LIVE IT OUT

So how do you find hope? Information alone can't do it. Let Jesus, the source of hope, transform you.

▶ **Identify a circumstance that leaves you feeling powerless.** As you enter that circumstance pray, "Jesus, please show me what to say and do."

▶ **Recognize Jesus' trustworthiness.** Identify several things in which you place your trust. Consider how Jesus is more trustworthy than each of those.

▶ **Find someone who needs hope.** Show Jesus' love through a kind gesture. Identify Jesus as the one who taught you how to be kind.

Can we ever truly find hope? Yes. Not only can we find it but we can experience it every day. **Call off the search party. We've found our true hope in Jesus Christ.**

Don't Waste Your Life

Last time I checked, 10 out of 10 people die. Death is certain. But people don't want to talk about it. Why? Let's face it: We fear it. And besides, it's flat-out uncomfortable and depressing to talk about our eventual demise. So what do we do instead? Author Os Guinness explains: "We are reluctant, even afraid, to admit that we all, without exception, will die. We surround ourselves with entertaining distractions so we don't have to think about death. We tranquilize ourselves with the trivial."

To continue reading "Don't Waste Your Life" from *HomeLife* magazine, visit *BibleStudiesforLife.com/articles*.

My group's prayer requests

....

....

....

....

....

....

....

....

My thoughts Tomorrow is not promised "Don't waste your life away".

SESSION 3

HOPE PERSONIFIED

Who is your favorite TV dad? Why?

QUESTION #1

LET H

God welcomes us because of His deep love for us.

THE BIBLE MEETS LIFE

The 20th century was full of honorable TV dads. Many times the dad was the centerpiece of the show, the staple of everything wholesome. These father figures sent out a clear message: a real dad acts like this.

Similarly, one of the clearest messages in the Bible is that God is our Father. But to some of us, that does not sound like good news. All fathers are flawed—despite the typical TV dad depiction—and some have caused great damage in the lives of their children. Consequently, our experience with our dads shapes how we see God as Father.

If Dad was the provider, you may go to God only when you want something. If Dad nurtured you, perhaps you approach God when you're hurting. If Dad was the disciplinarian, you might expect rebuke or correction from God. If Dad was absent, you might expect the same from God.

Jesus' teaching in Luke 15 shows just how great a Father God is. His story can change our whole understanding of what a father should be. It gives a face to what hope looks like.

WHAT DOES THE BIBLE SAY?

Luke 15:11-12, 20-24 *(HCSB)*

11 He also said: "A man had two sons.

12 The younger of them said to his father, 'Father, give me the share of the estate I have coming to me.' So he distributed the assets to them.

20 So he got up and went to his father. But while the son was still a long way off, his father saw him and was filled with compassion. He ran, threw his arms around his neck, and kissed him.

21 The son said to him, 'Father, I have sinned against heaven and in your sight. I'm no longer worthy to be called your son.'

22 "But the father told his slaves, 'Quick! Bring out the best robe and put it on him; put a ring on his finger and sandals on his feet.

23 Then bring the fattened calf and slaughter it, and let's celebrate with a feast,

24 because this son of mine was dead and is alive again; he was lost and is found!' So they began to celebrate.

Key Word

assets (v. 12)—Translates the Greek word, *bios,* that literally means "life." Here, the word implies one's livelihood or life's holdings, so therefore, his property.

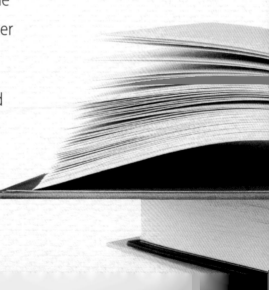

Luke 15:11-12

Through the prodigal son, Jesus revealed the heart of God in a story about a dad and his youngest son.

The son came to his father and said, "I want my inheritance." This may not seem like that big a deal, but the son wanted his inheritance right away. The only way for a son to get his inheritance was for his father to die. So the son was saying, "Your money means more to me than having a relationship with you."

Paraphrase: I wish you were dead.

The amazing thing is how the father responded. He said, "OK."

The father didn't try to manipulate his son into staying. Neither did he resort to guilt tactics. The father loved his son so much that he didn't encroach on his freedom. He let the son walk away.

▶ We all can be like the younger son. Our younger-son moments happen when we want the gifts God offers more than we want a relationship with Him.

▶ Or our younger-son moments happen when we take the gifts God gives us and use them selfishly. Selfishness brings results that damage us and those around us.

Consider some of the gifts that often come to us from the hand of God: wealth, romance, and power. These things aren't bad in and of themselves. But we often want these things more than we want God. Or we disobey God in the way we use them; we use them in ways that go against the character of God. When we make destructive choices, we move away from God's heart for us. In His love, God doesn't manipulate us or force us to stay. He gives us our freedom.

> *Since God is good, why do we often choose our own course instead of His?*

QUESTION #2

The younger son started his journey as a prince but made himself a slave. Everything he needed was provided by people who loved him. Due to his choices he ended up with no money, no friends, and no job. To illustrate how far a person can fall, the young man in Jesus' story became a servant … to pigs. In Jewish culture handling pigs or pork products was forbidden, and yet this young man became so desperate he ate the leftover food the pigs didn't want.

COME **HOME**

What counsel would you offer to a "prodigal son" in response to one of these statements they might make?

"My friends or family won't take me back."

"I don't think the damage can be undone."

"I've kept up the charade so long that I don't know how to stop."

"How do I even begin to approach God after what I've done?"

Luke 15:13-21

The prodigal son earned his PhD from the school of hard knocks with an emphasis on consequences. He, like we sometimes are, was determined to make choices that would ruin his life. Jesus didn't go into detail regarding those choices; He just referred to it as "foolish living." This phrase may mean "without restraint," meaning he indulged wherever his appetites took him, whenever they took him there, and without the wisdom of God.

Living this way never ends well for anyone. "Foolish living" brings less living and more pain. This pain is totally avoidable.

He had hit rock bottom.

▶ People who hit rock bottom feel like they have gone as low as they can possibly go and have no way to go but up.

▶ Rock bottom is the place we know we cannot stay.

▶ Rock bottom isn't limited to being almost dead, lying in a gutter, rotting from disease, and with a wallet full of debt. Rock bottom is the point you become willing to ask for help.

▶ Unfortunately when some people hit rock bottom they stay there. Why? Because they've lost hope.

Rock bottom is where our guilt and shame are likely to be strongest. Surrounded by pigs, the younger son was the Jewish picture of rock bottom. It was at this time he reached out for true help.

He was in financial need, he was in physical need, and he was in spiritual need. The young man knew he needed help. He chose the one good option he had left: to get up and go home.

> **What do these verses teach us about God as our Father?**
>
> QUESTION **#3**

When have you been extravagantly loved or forgiven?

QUESTION #4

Luke 15:22-24

The younger son headed home with a humble plan. He recognized that being a slave under his gracious father was far better than being a slave under anyone else. The son even prepared a little speech. It was not a grand speech, but it was an honest one.

How would his father respond? The younger son knew something of his father's character, but he failed to grasp how deep the father's love was for him. To fully appreciate just how loving this father was, consider that "an eye for an eye and a tooth for a tooth" was part of Jewish law and culture (see Matt. 5:38). Punishment was not to exceed the crime, but punishment was still expected to be apportioned.

As the younger son approached, you could imagine his shock when he saw his dad running to him.

When a heart is ready to come home, God doesn't walk to meet us; He runs to meet us.

Before the son could voice his little speech, this jubilant father threw the family cloak over his son's starving frame. The son stated his speech, but the father began preparations for a party. One gigantic "Welcome Home" party.

When we repent in any area of our lives, we can always find our hope in God. He is willing to forgive and to redeem. The love and grace of our Father are shocking. They should serve as a reminder that our God is like no other. There is none like Him. None.

How can we celebrate someone who embraces hope and comes back to the Father?

QUESTION #5

LIVE IT OUT

So how do you respond to God's welcome home?

▶ **Go home.** If you've been keeping your distance from God, return to Him. Begin praying daily and reading your Bible, too. God will show you the way back.

▶ **Forgive generously.** When was the last time you ran to forgive someone? Forgive even if it seems strange and shocking to everyone else around. Forgive as God has forgiven you. Let that someone know you've forgiven him or her.

▶ **Invite someone home.** Engage in an honest—but loving—conversation with "a prodigal." Patiently walk with this person as he or she finds the way to the Father.

The Father's "Welcome Home" sign is on display. **Come home to Him.**

A Father's Heart

Having been adopted, Glenn McClure felt like part of his journey was finding his birth family, as well as a biological daughter he fathered when he was 17 but had never met. "Both of those invitations from God felt extremely risky," McClure explains, "but those journeys powerfully demonstrated the Father's heart and love to me in a way that I never understood. It was transforming. I met my daughter Paula nine years ago (she was 18) and met my biological family seven years ago."

To continue reading "A Father's Heart" from *ParentLife* magazine, visit *BibleStudiesforLife.com/articles*.

My group's prayer requests

....
....
....
....
....
....
....
....
....
....

My thoughts

SESSION 4

HOPE EXPRESSED

Who is the most thankful person you know?

QUESTION #1

> *Gratitude is our response to the hope we have in Christ.*

THE BIBLE MEETS LIFE

In 2012, a superstorm devastated the northeast corner of the U.S. leaving many people without a home. Carey, a 31-year-old single mother, was one of those people.

One day as she was searching for clothes for her toddler in a local thrift store, a man approached with a handful of $100 bills. His words? "Don't give up hope. It's going to be OK."

Carey broke down. With tears in her eyes, she hugged the stranger. The moment changed her life forever—not because of her current needs but because it filled her with hope when she had none left. The mysterious stranger? He's a wealthy businessman who travels to cities affected by natural disasters giving out cash to those in need. He says it's his form of giving back.

What does it look like when you're filled with hope? When hope is expressed, it looks like gratitude. Sometimes it's small acts of kindness; other times it's big ones. In Psalm 138, King David expresses his hope in God. David resonates with gratitude.

WHAT DOES THE BIBLE SAY?

Psalm 138:1-8 *(HCSB)*

1 I will give You thanks with all my heart; I will sing Your praise before the heavenly beings.

2 I will bow down toward Your holy temple and give thanks to Your name for Your constant love and truth. You have exalted Your name and Your promise above everything else.

3 On the day I called, You answered me; You increased strength within me.

4 All the kings on earth will give You thanks, Lord, when they hear what You have promised.

5 They will sing of the Lord's ways, for the Lord's glory is great.

6 Though the Lord is exalted, He takes note of the humble; but He knows the haughty from a distance.

7 If I walk into the thick of danger, You will preserve my life from the anger of my enemies. You will extend Your hand; Your right hand will save me.

8 The Lord will fulfill His purpose for me. Lord, Your love is eternal; do not abandon the work of Your hands.

Key Words

heavenly beings (v. 1)—Scripture denies the existence of other gods; but it recognizes "gods" are treated as real by those who worship them.

takes note of (v. 6)—The point is that the supreme God of the universe is willing to consider the affairs of humans.

Psalm 138:1-3

Some things inevitably go together. For example, you automatically close your eyes when you sneeze. Have you ever tried to sneeze with your eyes open? Most people can't do it—even though it's not true that your eyeballs will pop out if you do! The reflexes involved in sneezing demand that you close your eyes.

In the same way, praise and gratitude automatically go together. It's impossible to give praise *to* God without being grateful *for* God. Psalm 138 captures a moment of authentic praise *and* gratitude.

"I'm in love! I'm in love! And I don't care who knows it!" That's the expression of love we see in films. David is not ashamed to share a similar feeling in his praise of God. David shouted out, " I will give You thanks with all my heart; I will sing Your praise before the heavenly beings."

We see here three elements of praise:

1. **Passion.** Notice the emphatic nature of David's praise. His praise and thanks were expressed with all his heart.

2. **Openness.** David didn't express his praise privately. He had an audience, and he was willing to expose his heart for God before anyone and everyone.

3. **Expression.** David wrote. He sang. He shouted. He bowed. David engaged his whole being in his praise of God.

What was David grateful for? David was thankful for who God is and for what God has said. He was thankful for God's character and because God had revealed His character to His people.

We often assume that people know we're grateful for them, but we need to express that gratitude. When it comes to expressing thanks to God, He obviously knows we're grateful whether we express it or not. We need to follow David's example and express our gratitude to God. This helps us keep everything in perspective. My gratitude is a reminder to myself of Who is the source of all I have.

> **What are the benefits of outwardly expressing our gratitude to God?**
>
> QUESTION #2

GRATITUDE IN ACTION

To personalize your gratefulness to God, read Psalm 138:1-3.
Then express it in your own words:

Verse 1: "I will give You thanks with all my heart;
I will sing Your praise before the heavenly beings."

....

....

....

Verse 2: "I will bow down toward Your holy temple and give thanks to Your name
for Your constant love and truth. You have exalted Your name and
Your promise above everything else."

....

....

....

Verse 3: "On the day I called, You answered me; You increased strength within me."

....

....

....

Psalm 138:4-6

"All the kings on earth will give You thanks, LORD."

Sure, it's easy to be grateful when you're a king. You're in charge. You have money. Everything is going well for you! That's not how my life is.

Project 7 is a company that donates more than 50 percent of its profits from the sales of bottled water, gum, mints, and coffee to help meet seven critical needs all over the world. Tyler Merrick, founder and CEO, once encouraged his friends to consider that others may look at our lives and see their dream job, their dream house, their dream life. No matter how bad our day may be, someone would gladly trade his life for ours. To another, our life seems to be like that of a king.

The wisest kings realize they serve One who is greater. Kings and others in high positions can praise God because they recognize His glory. The same can be said for those who may be at the opposite end of the spectrum. God "takes note of the humble." Humility and lowliness have to do with the posture of the heart toward God.

But gratitude fades when you begin to take for granted what God has given or done in your life. You might even think He owes those gifts to you. You would then take on an entitlement attitude. Whenever you feel entitled to have what you have, you can't be grateful for it. As long as you feel that what you have—or what you should have—is due you, you won't be grateful to God.

When I arrived home one day, I saw my kids' bikes lying in the driveway so that I couldn't park in the garage. I got so angry and was ready to tell them a thing or two. But then God reminded me that my life was a gift. Not only did I have kids who loved me, but I had a nice house ... and I even had a house for my car (a garage). Expressing gratitude and having the discipline to remain in a state of praise helps ward off these enemies of gratitude.

What are some things people in your stage of life feel entitled to?

QUESTION #3

When has someone protected you without
your awareness at the time?

QUESTION #4

Psalm 138:7-8

Verses 7-8 point to God's protection. When we're being protected we don't usually notice it. Every day parents protect their children in ways that go unnoticed by the children. God continually protects us in ways we don't notice. David said in verse 7, "If I walk into the thick of danger, You will preserve my life."

There are two types of protection: During rescue someone carries you out of harms way, or keeps you out of harm's way. During equipping someone makes you strong enough to face obstacles.

The more we become aware of the gifts, opportunities, and protection God gives, the more grateful we become and the more naturally we praise Him. The reality is that, no matter who we are or no matter what we've done, God's kindness shines on us. God's mercy and His graciousness is on us all.

God protected David from the wrath of his enemies. David experienced God's protection from both hostile nations and individual foes. We face equally dangerous enemies such as greed, jealousy, and pride. God works on our behalf against the forces of evil that lurk around us and the sinful desires within us.

Verse 8 explains the "why" behind God's protection and provision. Certainly, God protects and provides for us because of His love and kindness toward us. But God also works on my behalf to "fulfill His purpose for me." God provides for us so that we can do what He created us to do. As the apostle Paul said, "For we are His creation, created in Christ Jesus for good works, which God prepared ahead of time so that we should walk in them" (Eph. 2:10).

What can you point to as evidence that
God has not abandoned you?

QUESTION #5

LIVE IT OUT

How can gratitude grounded in hope be part of your life this week?

▶ **Record it.** Gratitude is a discipline. Once a day create a list that reads: "I am grateful for ___ today." See how this simple act shapes your mindset about God's provision. Use the journal space on the next page for the first list.

▶ **Say it.** Let gratitude permeate your conversations by speaking about what you are grateful for, rather than whining about how you wish things had gone.

▶ **Share it.** Choose someone to love for Jesus' sake. Do something this week that clearly communicates your gratitude to God: a gift or an act of service.

What does it look like when you're filled with hope? Hope looks like gratitude. **Each morning, thank God by finding a simple way to meet another's need.**

Joy in the Journey

I used to date a girl we'll call Gelda. This girl had the ability to suck the life out of any conversation with manipulation or sulking. The funny thing is that when we were dating, I was praying to God that He would bring us closer together, that He would allow us to up our level of commitment.

To continue reading "Joy in the Journey" from *HomeLife* magazine, visit *BibleStudiesforLife.com/articles*.

My group's prayer requests

_____

_____

_____

_____

_____

_____

_____

_____

_____

My thoughts

SESSION 5

HOPE RENEWED

What are different ways people respond to failure?

> *When you fail, Jesus will restore you.*

THE BIBLE MEETS LIFE

Failure is painful. It's that moment we fall flat on our faces, we make a fool of ourselves, or we betray our values. Failure can also be the cause when things don't go quite the way we had hoped.

There are generally two types of failure:

1. **You do something you don't realize is wrong.** Perhaps you make a right turn at a stoplight when you didn't see the "No Right on Red" sign. These failures are also mistakes. You failed to see the sign. (The police officer may extend grace, but he has the right to issue a ticket.)

2. **You know what is right, but you don't do it.** You deliberately choose the wrong course, or choose to not travel the right course. This isn't a mistake, it's a sin.

We all fall short. We all sin. So then the question isn't *if* we're going to fail, but what are we going to do *when* we fail. Two key moments in the life of Peter give us the answer.

WHAT DOES THE BIBLE SAY?

John 18:15-18, 25-27; 21:15-19 *(HCSB)*

18:15 Meanwhile, Simon Peter was following Jesus, as was another disciple. That disciple was an acquaintance of the high priest; so he went with Jesus into the high priest's courtyard. **16** But Peter remained standing outside by the door. So the other disciple, the one known to the high priest, went out and spoke to the girl who was the doorkeeper and brought Peter in. **17** Then the slave girl who was the doorkeeper said to Peter, "You aren't one of this man's disciples too, are you?" "I am not!" he said. **18** Now the slaves and the temple police had made a charcoal fire, because it was cold. They were standing there warming themselves, and Peter was standing with them, warming himself.

25 Now Simon Peter was standing and warming himself. They said to him, "You aren't one of His disciples too, are you?" He denied it and said, "I am not!" **26** One of the high priest's slaves, a relative of the man whose ear Peter had cut off, said, "Didn't I see you with Him in the garden?" **27** Peter then denied it again. Immediately a rooster crowed.

21:15 When they had eaten breakfast, Jesus asked Simon Peter, "Simon, son of John, do you love Me more than these?" "Yes, Lord," he said to Him, "You know that I love You." "Feed My lambs," He told him. **16** A second time He asked him, "Simon, son of John, do you love Me?" "Yes, Lord," he said to Him, "You know that I love You." "Shepherd My sheep," He told him. **17** He asked him the third time, "Simon, son of John, do you love Me?" Peter was grieved that He asked him the third time, "Do you love Me?" He said, "Lord, You know everything! You know that I love You." "Feed My sheep," Jesus said. **18** "I assure you: When you were young, you would tie your belt and walk wherever you wanted. But when you grow old, you will stretch out your hands and someone else will tie you and carry you where you don't want to go." **19** He said this to signify by what kind of death he would glorify God. After saying this, He told him, "Follow Me!"

John 18:15-18,25-27

John 18 recounts what had to be the worst moments in Peter's life. Peter had no idea how these events would turn out. Jesus had been arrested. John and Peter followed the arresting party to the residence of the high priest. John, known by the high priest, was able to move in closer. Peter stayed outside the gate until John could send a servant girl to let him in. The young girl who guarded the door quizzed Peter, perhaps even as he entered the courtyard, "You aren't one of this man's disciples too, are you?"

How should Peter answer? If he said, "Yes," she could turn him in. Now was Peter's moment to be brave. Instead, Peter, one of the inner circle of disciples, the one who bravely walked on water, said, "I am not!"

Two more times, people asked Peter if he knew Jesus. The third time, the question came from a man related to the guy whose ear Peter had cut off earlier that night (John 18:10). That scared Peter so badly he even cursed as he swore, "I don't know this man you're talking about!" (Mark 14:71).

Three denials. Then the rooster crowed.

We tend to see the men and women in Scripture as bigger than life. Their encounters with God and their victories seem so far beyond what we experience today. We may view their failures as equally above ours … and more catastrophic. Consequently, we might be tempted to say: "I would never fail Jesus like that."

That's just what Peter had said earlier that night. When Jesus shared one last meal with His disciples, Jesus predicted Judas's betrayal. Peter declared that he would lay down his life for Jesus. Jesus explained that Peter would betray Him. Peter's betrayal would come in the form of denial (John 13:37-38). This must have come as a shock to Peter. He was the first of the disciples to confess, "You are the Messiah, the Son of the living God" (Matt. 16:16). Peter responded like many of us would: "I will never deny You" (Matt. 26:35)!

> *How do you respond to Peter's fear of being identified with Jesus?*
>
> QUESTION #2

> *How do we deal with the shame of repeated failure?*
>
> QUESTION #3

John 21:15-19

Maybe we're not so different from Peter after all. We have all been in circumstances where we have given in to fear or succumbed to the crowd and denied Jesus in one way or another. We've had our own moments when we tried to hide our relationship to Him.

Thankfully, we are not left in our failures. When we fail, Jesus will restore us.

HOPE SINGS

Share a line from a Christian song, hymn, or chorus that has given you hope:

....

....

....

What about this line gives you hope?

....

....

....

For an example, listen to Mandisa's "He Will Come" from the album *True Beauty* (Sparrow, 2007). Search MandisaOfficial.com/home/music/ for "True Beauty by Mandisa," or scan this QR Code.

In the early verses of John 21 we discover that Peter and six others went fishing. They had encountered the resurrected Jesus, but what were they to do now? Peter returned to doing what he knew: fishing.

A man appeared on the shore and called out to them, asking if they had caught any fish. They hadn't. The man encouraged them to cast their net on the other side of the boat.

When the men followed those instructions, the net became so full of fish they couldn't haul it in. This event was similar to what Jesus had done for Peter in one of His earliest encounters with him (Luke 5:4-7). The connection became clear to John, who shouted, "It is the Lord!"

Peter apparently made the same connection, for Peter jumped into the water and swam to shore to meet Jesus. Peter appeared delighted to see Jesus again, but I wonder if there were moments of awkwardness. After all, the boastful Peter had humiliated himself by his denial. Jesus had returned to Peter and spoken to him with no mention of his failures. But Peter likely recalled those failures. Even if Peter felt forgiven, he may not have felt restored.

After the meal Jesus and Peter had a conversation during which Jesus asked Peter three times if Peter loved Him. Each time Peter gave an emphatic yes. Jesus responded by telling the apostle to take care of His sheep.

> *What is your emotional reaction to the events in this passage? Why?*

QUESTION #4

"Time doesn't heal all wounds; God heals wounds."

—PETE WILSON

Jesus asked His question three times. Peter had denied the Lord three times. Jesus invited Peter three times to return to His calling. Jesus' point was not on Peter's shortcomings; Jesus' emphasis was on forgiveness and restoration. Restoration has two parts.

1. **Your past is forgiven.** The beginning of forgiveness is the decision to not seek vengeance. Jesus could have been angry with Peter, could have held a grudge, or worse. Yet Jesus did none of these things. Jesus chose to forgive Peter, and He chooses to forgive us. "While we were still sinners, Christ died for us" (Rom. 5:8).

   Jesus knows every betrayal we've ever made and ever will make; yet He still loves us. It's in Jesus' sacrifice on the cross that we find hope for forgiveness.

2. **Your future is radically changed.** Jesus called Peter into a future of serving and loving people. Peter, a man others considered "uneducated and untrained" (Acts 4:13), went on to become one of the most influential spiritual leaders in history. Through the life, leadership, and writings of Peter, God did a great work in spreading the message of Christ.

> *How can we help each other when we stumble or fail?*

QUESTION #5

LIVE IT OUT

How does Jesus' promise of restoration and renewed hope affect you?

▶ **Be honest.** Pray and ask the Holy Spirit to reveal your sins and failures. Turn from them and receive God's forgiveness.

▶ **Seek reconciliation.** If your sin has hurt other people, humbly ask for their forgiveness. Follow God's leadership to repair any damage you've caused.

▶ **Foster reconciliation in someone.** Listen as someone tells you about a failure. Pray together for God's restoration. Implement that restoration together.

Failure is painful, but it doesn't have to be fatal. With Christ, failures can lead to the beginning of something new. **It's time to let Jesus restore you and replace your failures with hope.**

Do You Make the Grade?

Report cards. For some, the memory evokes dread—a scheduled reminder of academic shortcomings. A few C's meant getting grounded or, at the very least, receiving that disapproving look from parents. Self-worth often became embedded in those weighty letters. Right or wrong, the report card system brands a certain scale into our lives: perfect, almost perfect, average, below average, and failing. Although report cards often are only a childhood reality, the concept infiltrates our adult lives, including our spirituality.

To continue reading "Do You Make the Grade?" from *HomeLife* magazine, visit *BibleStudiesforLife.com/articles*.

My group's prayer requests

....

....

....

....

....

....

....

....

....

My thoughts

SESSION 6

HOPE SHARED

What is something you had to share when you were growing up?

QUESTION #1

#BSFLshared

*After finding hope in Christ,
we must share it with others.*

THE BIBLE MEETS LIFE

Sharing can be difficult. For example, sharing that one last slice of dessert is a challenge. As a child, sharing a bed with a sibling (or two) often translated into more crowding and less sleep.

But sharing doesn't always mean less. Sharing a good book or movie doesn't diminish our experience; it gives us something to talk about and provides fresh perspective.

Hope is also something we can share without losing. When hope takes a foothold in our lives, it affects our actions, our words, our attitudes, even our emotions. When people seeking joy or hope encounter you, they notice your hope. They can be drawn to it.

The Bible gives us the story of Peter and John's interaction with a crippled beggar. They had no money or resources to give but they had hope in Christ. The way they shared that hope changed the man's life forever.

WHAT DOES THE BIBLE SAY?

Acts 3:1-10 *(HCSB)*

1 Now Peter and John were going up together to the temple complex at the hour of prayer at three in the afternoon.

2 And a man who was lame from birth was carried there and placed every day at the temple gate called Beautiful, so he could beg from those entering the temple complex.

3 When he saw Peter and John about to enter the temple complex, he asked for help.

4 Peter, along with John, looked at him intently and said, "Look at us."

5 So he turned to them, expecting to get something from them.

6 But Peter said, "I don't have silver or gold, but what I have, I give you: In the name of Jesus Christ the Nazarene, get up and walk!"

7 Then, taking him by the right hand he raised him up, and at once his feet and ankles became strong.

8 So he jumped up, stood, and started to walk, and he entered the temple complex with them—walking, leaping, and praising God.

9 All the people saw him walking and praising God,

10 and they recognized that he was the one who used to sit and beg at the Beautiful Gate of the temple complex. So they were filled with awe and astonishment at what had happened to him.

Key Words

the hour of prayer (v. 1)—One of two regular daily times of prayer accompanying temple sacrifices, morning and afternoon. This reference is to the prayer "at three in the afternoon."

awe and astonishment (v. 10)—Temple regulars knew of the man's handicap. The response to the mans healing was astonishment (in Greek *ekstasis,* from which comes our English, "ecstasy").

Acts 3:1-4

Acts 3 tells of an otherwise typical day for Peter and John. It was 3 p.m. and they were headed to the temple at the hour of prayer. They weren't necessarily on a mission to heal anyone. They were just going about their routines.

That's the thing about loving and serving others. Many times we don't have to go looking for those opportunities. Many times God brings them to us. The questions are:

▶ Will we have the eyes to see the need before us?

▶ Will we have the courage to do what God calls us to do?

Verse 2 introduces us to a man who might have been easy to miss. He was a man who sat at the same place at the same time every day. He had been lame from birth and had been carried to that place so he could beg for handouts from the large crowd coming to the temple. Perhaps people had conditioned themselves to ignore people like him. When he saw Peter and John and asked them for help, he may not have expected much from them. At best, a coin. At worst, a rude comment as their robes brushed by.

Peter and John did not ignore the man. Quite the opposite. Verse 4 notes that they looked at him intently. Looking fully at someone means giving him enough attention, time, and energy to really understand him and his needs. Peter and John not only looked at the man, but they called on him to do the same. "Look at us."

The man, lame from birth, likely didn't have a clue who Peter and John were, except … maybe … men with pockets full of money. His request was for financial help (v. 3-6). The fact that the lame man misunderstood Peter and John didn't stop them from serving him. It's not up to us to discern the motives of those who want our help. It's only up to us to help.

> *How can we discern the less obvious needs of others?*

QUESTION #2

SHARING HOPE

Mark yourself on the scales.

I WANT TO SHARE HOPE

I love talking about Christ's hope.

10

5

0

Hope is a private thing.

I KNOW HOW TO SHARE HOPE

I share Christ's hope in words and actions.

10

5

0

I don't know how to share hope.

Acts 3:5-8

If someone has lost hope, what can I do? What do I have to offer?

▶ Will I have the time or energy to serve?

▶ How will I make this whole offering hope to others thing work?

▶ Do they even want what I have to offer?

The first words Peter said to the man must have seemed more than a little discouraging: "I don't have silver or gold." I can imagine the man thinking, *Great. Then move along and stop wasting my time.*

The man thought he needed money. Typically, the thing we think we need is only a symptom of a greater problem. The man's need for money was a symptom of his physical disability which kept him from working. The lame man wanted something to get him through the day, yet he was talking to men who could help him walk again.

What Peter and John had to offer the man was a sure hope and confidence in the presence and power of Christ. We may not possess the power to command a lame man to stand up and walk, but we have the same hope and confidence in the presence and power of Christ. And we can share it.

> *What obstacles or excuses keep us from serving people and offering hope?*
>
> QUESTION #3

Whom has God placed in your life? What do they need to hear you say or see you do? You have more to offer than you think you do. You can share the hope you have. That may take courage. God will provide it. Courage isn't when you feel brave; it's when you do the right thing regardless of how you feel.

▶ It takes courage to notice others.

▶ It takes courage to evaluate the resources you have.

▶ It takes courage to step from inaction to action, to serve others.

QUESTION #4

Peter and John healed in Jesus' name. How can we meet the needs of others so that it clearly points to God?

When we step out in faith to serve others with all that God has given us, amazing things start to happen. Healing begins to take place in both ourselves and in others. We become conduits of God's grace to others. Our impact in the world becomes exponential; the effect grows greater than we ever could have imagined.

Peter told the lame man, "In the name of Jesus Christ the Nazarene, get up and walk!" Peter reached down and helped the lame man up. As he did, the man's feet and ankles became strong. He jumped up. But that's not all he did. He began to jump and praise God in the temple courts.

Acts 3:9-10

Healing the lame man wasn't the end; it was only the beginning. Remember that it was 3 p.m. and the temple complex was crowded with people gathered for prayer. They all saw this man who was now healed, and they "were filled with awe and astonishment at what had happened to him." The miracle wasn't just about the man; it was about the community.

Part of the thrill of serving others is seeing the ripple effects that occur in that person's life as well as our own. Sharing hope with one person has a way of spreading. The reality is that our choices—for better or worse—have a ripple effect that we may never fully understand.

You have hope in Christ. As you have received hope, offer it to others as much as possible in as many ways as possible. To engage in this adventure is to embark in the only calling worthy of our lives. It's a calling of hope.

How have you witnessed the ripple effect of helping someone in a small way that impacted others in a big way?

QUESTION #5

LIVE IT OUT

So what does finding hope look like as you share it with others?

▶ **Open your eyes.** Take time each day to pray a simple but powerful prayer: "God, make me aware of those around me who may not know You."

▶ **Open your home.** As you become aware of people who are not Christ followers, establish relationships with them. Let them see Jesus in you. Invite them over to share a meal.

▶ **Open your mouth.** Share your story of hope with a friend or coworker. How has Jesus brought you through a rough time?

God gave you hope when He healed your past through Jesus Christ. Like Peter and John's interaction with the beggar, you've got something worth sharing. **You may never know the ripple effect you start with a little bit of hope.**

Reaching Beyond the Beach

Though her youthful voice confirms her still tender age, Georgia Cook articulates her perspective on God, relationships, and profession with the maturity of a young adult. But then again, Georgia is not a normal kid.

To continue reading "Reaching Beyond the Beach" from *ParentLife* magazine, visit *BibleStudiesforLife.com/articles*.

My group's prayer requests

My thoughts

Let Hope In

We are never beyond or outside of hope. We have seen through the pages of Scripture that we can find hope. That hope is in Jesus, who is the absolute personification of hope. We can maintain that hope amid failure, in spite of our past, and during circumstances beyond our control. That's a sure hope.

Christ

We are all without hope, but Christ meets us in our hopelessness, forgives our past, removes our sins, and gives us a new, abundant, eternal life. We have a sure and certain hope because of Jesus Christ.

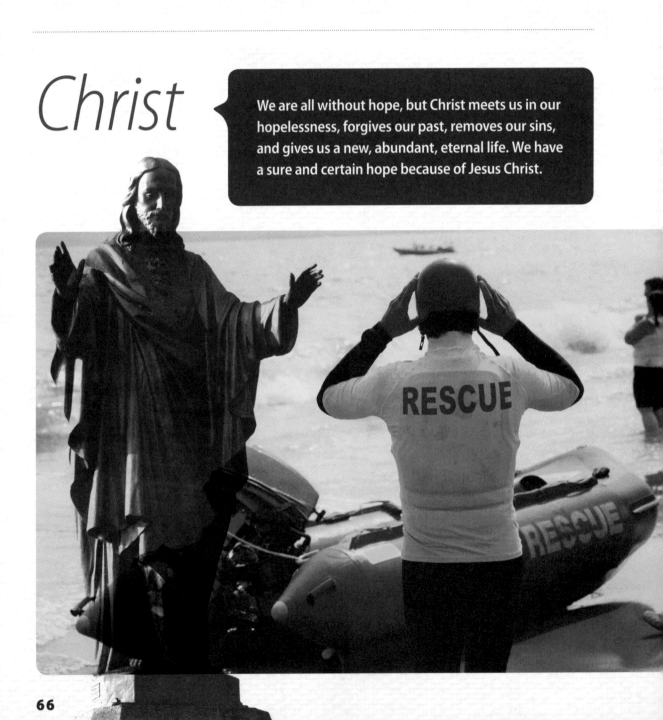

Community

Many believers have relegated hope to spending a future in heaven. They have hope and confidence that they will go to heaven when they die, but they have lost hope for how they live now. Believers who live such defeated lives need other believers to walk alongside them, showing that the hope they have in Christ is a hope for today.

Culture

Those around us will only know hope if we share it with them. The world can know what a sure and certain hope is when they see it in us. When we point them to Christ, we point them to hope. In Christ, they then can walk victoriously.

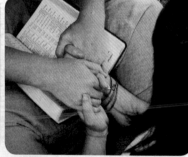

LEADER GUIDE

LET HOPE IN

GENERAL INSTRUCTIONS

In order to make the most of this study and to ensure a richer group experience, it's recommended that all group participants read through the teaching and discussion content in full before each group meeting. As a leader, it is also a good idea for you to be familiar with this content and prepared to summarize it for your group members as you move through the material each week.

Each session of the Bible study is made up of three sections:

1. THE BIBLE MEETS LIFE.

An introduction to the theme of the session and its connection to everyday life, along with a brief overview of the primary Scripture text. This section also includes an icebreaker question or activity.

2. WHAT DOES THE BIBLE SAY?

This comprises the bulk of each session and includes the primary Scripture text along with explanations for key words and ideas within that text. This section also includes most of the content designed to produce and maintain discussion within the group.

3. LIVE IT OUT.

The final section focuses on application, using bulleted summary statements to answer the question, *So what?* As the leader, be prepared to challenge the group to apply what they learned during the discussion by transforming it into action throughout the week.

For group leaders, the *Let Hope In* Leader Guide contains several features and tools designed to help you lead participants through the material provided.

QUESTION 1—ICEBREAKER

These opening questions and/or activities are designed to help participants transition into the study and begin engaging the primary themes to be discussed. Be sure everyone has a chance to speak, but maintain a low-pressure environment.

DISCUSSION QUESTIONS

Each "What Does the Bible Say?" section features at least three questions designed to spark discussion and interaction within your group. These questions encourage critical thinking, so be sure to allow a period of silence for participants to process the question and form an answer.

The *Let Hope In* Leader Guide also contains follow-up questions and optional activities that may be helpful to your group, if time permits.

DVD CONTENT

Each video features teaching from Pete Wilson on the primary themes found in the session. We recommend that you show this video in one of three places: (1) At the beginning of group time, (2) After the icebreaker, or (3) After a quick review and/or summary of "What Does the Bible Say?" A video summary is included as well. You may choose to use this summary as background preparation to help you guide the group.

The Leader Guide contains additional questions to help unpack the video and transition into the discussion. For a digital Leader Guide with commentary, see the "Leader Tools" folder on the DVD-ROM in your Leader Kit.

SESSION ONE: HOPE NEEDED

The Point: You are never beyond hope.

The Passage: 2 Samuel 9:6-13

The Setting: In 1 Samuel 20:14-17, Jonathan, the son of King Saul, made a covenant that ensured his family would remain under the faithful love and protection of David. Years later, when David was king and the family of Saul was removed from power, David honored that covenant by taking care of the crippled son of Jonathan.

QUESTION 1: What did you want to be when you grew up?

> *Optional activity:* Play a movie clip where characters seem to be in a hopeless situation, then discuss the following questions as a group. (Note: Be sure to choose a movie that is appropriate for your group.)
>
> • What emotions did you experience during that clip? Why?
>
> • What ideas or images come to mind when you hear the word *hopeless*?
>
> • What ideas or images come to mind when you hear the word *hope*?

Video Summary: The theme of this opening video session is that we all need hope. Pete shares the story of Mephibosheth and David from 2 Samuel 9:1-13. Mephibosheth was the grandson of Saul and son of David's dear friend Jonathan. After being crippled in an accident, Mephibosheth lived a reclusive life, isolated from everyone, full of shame, and void of hope. But this all changed when David rescued him, living out his love for his now deceased friend Jonathan. After his rescue, Mephibosheth was able to release himself from his past and refuse to cling to it any longer. He experienced freedom. He found hope.

WATCH THE DVD SEGMENT FOR SESSION 1, THEN USE THE FOLLOWING QUESTIONS AND DISCUSSION POINTS TO TRANSITION INTO THE STUDY.

• Mephibosheth had lots of clutter in his life that kept him from moving forward — things like his physical condition and his family background. What is your clutter? What are you clinging to from your past that has come to define who you are today?

• In his message Pete states: "If we don't learn how to let God transform our past, we will transfer it into other areas of our lives." In what ways have you seen this play out in your own life?

WHAT DOES THE BIBLE SAY?

ASK FOR A VOLUNTEER TO READ ALOUD 2 SAMUEL 9:6-13.

Response: What's your initial reaction to these verses?

• What do you like about the text?

• What questions do you have about these verses?

TURN THE GROUP'S ATTENTION TO 2 SAMUEL 9:6-7.

QUESTION 2: What was a circumstance that caused you to feel hopeless?

This question is included to help group members empathize with Mephibosheth and, perhaps, reconnect with their own seasons or moments of hopelessness.

Optional follow-up: How did you eventually find hope and move forward?

Optional activity: Ask group members to complete the activity "Looking Back" on page 11 of the group member book. Ask for volunteers to share their responses to one of the three situations listed.

MOVE TO 2 SAMUEL 9:8

QUESTION 3: Why is it difficult for people to let go of the past and move forward?

Identifying difficulties or barriers associated with letting go of the past should move group members along a continuum that culminates with discovering the hope we have in Christ.

CONTINUE WITH 2 SAMUEL 9:9-13.

QUESTION 4: When has God blessed you in an unexpected way?

This provides group members with an opportunity to tell a story. Be ready with an example of your own.

Optional follow-up: God does not offer us mercy on the basis of our worthiness. Name specific ways this is counter-intuitive to what we experience in our society today—in our careers, with friends, athletics, school, appearance, etc.

QUESTION 5: How does embracing hope change you and others?

Ultimately this is an application question. In answering, group members are making a case for embracing the hope we have been given.

Optional follow-up: What obstacles hinder or prevent us from embracing hope?

Note: The following question does not appear in the group member book. Use it in your group discussion as time allows.

QUESTION 6: How can we as a group help one another find and focus on hope?

Encourage group members to be honest about what they need from one another. A significant part of group life is support and accountability. Take this opportunity to reiterate the importance of both.

Optional follow-up: How can we promote the value of hope in God throughout our spheres of influence?

LIVE IT OUT

Mephibosheth suffered due to circumstances, sinful actions of others, and his own poor choices. But still he chose to embrace hope. Invite group members to consider these three actions they can take to do the same.

- **Appreciate a kindness.** Look around. How is God imparting hope to you through another person?

- **Forgive yourself.** What hurtful actions have you chosen that have brought you guilt and shame? Repent (turn from old ways), receive God's forgiveness, and start living with His hope.

- **Be an agent of hope to someone trapped by his or her past.** Offer genuine friendship and encouragement—minus any judgment. Unsure of what to say or do? Share the gospel. Imitate Christ's unconditional love in your speech and behavior.

Challenge: As you go about your week, keep an eye open for entertainment forms—books, movies, songs, TV shows, and so on—that try to push you toward hopelessness. Choose instead to thank God for the hope He's given you in those moments.

Pray: Ask for prayer requests and ask group members to pray for the different requests as intercessors. As the leader, close this time by committing the members of your group to the Lord and asking Him to help each of you remember that even when your past carries shame and regret, your future can be shaped by hope.

SESSION TWO: HOPE FOUND

The Point: When we seek Christ, we find hope.

The Passage: Matthew 8:1-13

The Setting: In Matthew 8, Jesus performed several miracles that demonstrated His authority. Two of the miracles—the healing of a man with a skin disease and the healing of a centurion's servant—also emphasized Jesus' compassion.

QUESTION 1: When have you lost something important to you?

> *Optional follow-up:* What emotions do you commonly experience in times of loss?

> *Optional activity:* Allow group members to play a "shell game" for several minutes. Start by placing three plastic cups and a rubber ball on a table or flat surface. One person hides the ball under a cup, then swaps the cups around several times. The other person attempts to follow the cup with the ball and then identify that cup after the shuffling is over.

> Encourage group members to take turns shuffling the cups and attempting to identify where the ball has gone. Wrap this time up by drawing a parallel between the game and the topic of seeking and finding.

Video Summary: In this video session, Pete talks about two stories from Matthew 8. First, how Jesus healed the man with leprosy, and second the dialogue between Jesus and the Roman soldier. These two stories represent two of the most despised groups of people of the time, but through their experiences we see that Jesus is willing to touch what is untouchable. He is willing to approach the unapproachable. Jesus accepts us in whatever condition we are in. Faith in Jesus is what unlocks the door to the kingdom. And when Jesus touches us, we will never be the same.

WATCH THE DVD SEGMENT FOR SESSION 2, THEN USE THE FOLLOWING QUESTIONS AND DISCUSSION POINTS TO TRANSITION INTO THE STUDY.

- Pete talks about how Jesus is comfortable in the midst of your mess. How comfortable are you with your mess? Explain.

- When you are broken and in need, to whom do you turn? Where do you go for help?

WHAT DOES THE BIBLE SAY?

ASK FOR A VOLUNTEER TO READ ALOUD MATTHEW 8:1-13.

Response: What's your initial reaction to these verses?

- What questions do you have about these verses?
- What do you hope to gain from studying how you can find hope?

TURN THE GROUP'S ATTENTION TO MATTHEW 8:1-4.

QUESTION 2: How might sin in our lives make us feel like a leper?

The purpose of this question is not to beat one another up. This session begins with this question as a means to acknowledge the proverbial "elephant in the room." Answering this question requires group members to consider how sin isolates us from God, those we love, and our true identities.

> ***Optional follow-up:*** How are these feelings impacted by the ways we choose to deal with our sin?

QUESTION 3: Why might someone think Jesus would be unwilling to help?

Answers will vary. Encourage the group to be transparent. Answers will help group members become more acquainted or familiar with their own understanding of who God is.

MOVE TO MATTHEW 8:5-9.

QUESTION 4: Since Jesus' authority is our only hope, why do we look for hope in other things or people?

You may begin by asking the group if they truly believe that Jesus is their only hope. This question asks group members to look deeper into what they really believe. It's an opportunity to discuss idols they may have established as well as matters of faith.

> ***Optional follow-up:*** Where does our culture encourage us to turn when we're in need of hope?

> ***Optional follow-up:*** How have you experienced these cultural sources of hope and found them wanting?

> ***Optional activity:*** Ask group members to complete the activity "What Hope Looks Like" on page 22 of the group member book. Ask for volunteers to share their responses.

CONTINUE WITH MATTHEW 8:10-13.

QUESTION 5: In your daily life, what is the evidence that you have hope in Christ?

This is an application question that invites members of the group to share their personal testimonies of hope.

> ***Optional follow-up:*** What obstacles keep you from more fully benefiting from that hope?

Note: The following question does not appear in the group member book. Use it in your group discussion as time allows.

QUESTION 6: What does it look like practically for us to "seek Christ"?

This question asks the group to paint a fairly narrow picture of "living in Christ." Point out the importance of the word *practically* since this asks them to consider their minute-to-minute, day-to-day lives—not just the big things.

Optional follow-up: What might God be calling you to surrender to Him in order to seek Him more fully?

LIVE IT OUT

So how do we find hope? Information alone can't do it. Encourage group members to let Jesus, the source of hope, transform them by calling their attention to these three actions they can take.

- **Identify a circumstance that leaves you feeling powerless.** As you enter that circumstance pray, "Jesus, please show me what to say and do."

- **Recognize Jesus' trustworthiness.** Identify several things in which you place your trust. Consider how Jesus is more trustworthy than each of those.

- **Find someone who needs hope.** Show Jesus' love through a kind gesture. Identify Jesus as the one who taught you how to be kind.

Challenge: Think this week of someone you know who may think he or she is unworthy to come to Jesus. Consider sharing insights with him or her on experiencing true hope in Christ with him or her.

Pray: Ask for prayer requests and ask group members to pray for the different requests as intercessors. As the leader, close this time by committing the members of your group to the Lord and asking Him to help each of you experience true hope every day.

SESSION THREE: HOPE PERSONIFIED

The Point: God welcomes us because of His deep love for us.

The Passage: Luke 15:11-12,20-24

The Setting: The religious leaders criticized Jesus, not because the tax collectors and sinners were coming to Him, but because He was welcoming them. Jesus told three parables to illustrate lostness and the importance God places on recovering those who are lost. His parable about the prodigal son illustrates how a loving Father welcomes any sinner who comes to Him.

QUESTION 1: Who is your favorite TV dad? Why?

Optional activity: Take the icebreaker question deeper by visually organizing the famous dads from TV. Ask for a volunteer to write down two categories on a whiteboard or large sheet of paper and label them "positive" and "negative." Then ask the volunteer to record the group's answers to the following questions based on those categories.

- Who are some current dads from movies and TV shows, and which category do they fall in?

- Who are some famous dads from past movies and TV shows, and which category do they fall in?

- Which of these dads do you like best? Why?

- What qualities do the dads in our two categories share?

Optional follow-up: How would you summarize the way dads are portrayed in current movies and TV shows?

Video Summary: In this video message, Pete looks at the relationship between a father and his sons in Luke 15:11-32, the story of the prodigal son. The younger son disrespected his father and his family by requesting his inheritance early, but the father honored his son's request. The father seemed more worried about his son than his own honor and reputation. The younger son took the money and left home. But he eventually returned, poor, needy, and desperate. His father ran to him, welcoming his youngest son back with open arms. When the father refused to turn his back on the younger son, the older son did some running of his own. And the father did the same thing he did with the younger son—he ran after him. What this father valued most was his relationship with his sons. Just like the father in this story—our Father desires a relationship with us no matter how far away we are.

WATCH THE DVD SEGMENT FOR SESSION 3, THEN USE THE FOLLOWING QUESTIONS AND DISCUSSION POINTS TO TRANSITION INTO THE STUDY.

- Pete talked about how sometimes we may feel that our sin disqualifies us from being loved by God. What aspects of this story help you see that isn't true?

- In Luke 15:11-32, the thing that most pleased the father was restored relationships with his sons. Are there areas of your relationship with your Father that need to be restored? What steps do you need to take to make that happen?

WHAT DOES THE BIBLE SAY?

ASK FOR A VOLUNTEER TO READ ALOUD LUKE 15:11-32.

Response: What's your initial reaction to these verses?

- What questions do you have about these verses?

- What new application do you hope to get from this passage?

TURN THE GROUP'S ATTENTION TO LUKE 15:11-12.

QUESTION 2: Since God is good, why do we often choose our own course instead of His?

What we say we believe isn't always the truest indicator of what we truly believe. The truest indicator of what we really believe is behavior. This question asks the group to consider how their behavior reveals what they really believe about God. We're beginning here to reinforce the point of this session: God welcomes us because of His deep love for us.

Optional follow-up: How do we tell which course is God's and which we are choosing on our own?

Optional activity: Encourage group members to complete the activity "Come Home" on page 31 of the group member book. Ask for volunteers to share their answers to one of the responses listed.

MOVE TO LUKE 15:13-21.

QUESTION 3: What do these verses teach us about God as our Father?

This is an interpretation question that asks each group member to give his or her interpretation, or understanding, of these verses.

Optional follow-up: How do these characteristics of God compare and contrast to those discussed in our icebreaker activity?

CONTINUE WITH LUKE 15:22-24.

QUESTION 4: When have you been extravagantly loved or forgiven?

Challenge the group to think about what is required to love or forgive extravagantly .

Optional follow-up: What emotions did you experience in those moments?

QUESTION 5: How can we celebrate someone who embraces hope and comes back to the Father?

You may also ask the group how they would recognize someone that has embraced hope and returned to the Father.

Note: The following question does not appear in the group member book. Use it in your group discussion as time allows.

QUESTION 6: What kinds of things keep us from accepting God's deep love for us?

Ultimately this question is about idolatry. We're asking the group to identify those things that prevent them from knowing the full breadth and depth of God's love for us.

LIVE IT OUT

So how do we respond to God's welcome home? Encourage group members to consider the following options:

- **Go home.** If you've been keeping your distance from God, return to Him. Begin praying daily and reading your Bible, too. God will show you the way back.

- **Forgive generously.** When was the last time you ran to forgive someone? Forgive even if it seems strange and shocking to everyone else around. Forgive as God has forgiven you. Let that someone know you've forgiven him or her.

- **Invite someone home.** Engage in an honest—but loving— conversation with "a prodigal." Patiently walk with this person as he or she finds the way to the Father.

Challenge: Everyone's perception of God is colored to some degree by their attitude and relationship with their father. Throughout the Bible, God is referred to as our Father. Jesus used an illustration of a father to help us grasp the depth of God the Father's love for us. Take some time this week to reflect on possible ways your relationship with your earthly father has colored your relationship with your heavenly Father. Then make a list of things you know to be true about your relationship with God.

Pray: Ask for prayer requests and ask group members to pray for the different requests as intercessors. As the leader, close this time by asking the Lord to help each of you remember and trust in the love your heavenly Father has for you.

SESSION FOUR: HOPE EXPRESSED

The Point: Gratitude is our response to the hope we have in Christ.

The Passage: Psalm 138:1-8

The Setting: We do not know when David wrote Psalm 138, but this Psalm reflects a lifetime of trust in God. God is exalted above all others, and He protected and delivered David in all circumstances. David expressed a thankfulness and trust that God would fulfill all His plans for David.

QUESTION 1: Who is the most thankful person you know?

> *Optional activity:* Help group members experience the emotions of thankfulness and gratitude by giving each of them a small gift—something inexpensive like candy or a hand-written card. After distributing these gifts, ask the following questions to unpack their feelings of gratitude.
>
> - Having received a small gift, what emotions are you experiencing now?
>
> - When you receive an unexpected gift, do you feel more grateful for the gift itself or for the knowledge that someone thought of you? Explain.
>
> - What are some of the gifts we have received from God?
>
> - How would you describe your emotional reaction to those gifts?

Video Summary: In this week's video message, Pete talks about Psalm 138 and responding to God with a grateful heart. We don't really know what was going on in David's life when he wrote this psalm, but we do know it represents a heart that has experienced God and is grateful. Gratitude is how we express our hope in God. Gratitude is not invisible. It isn't silent. When we are thankful for something or someone, we verbalize it—and that's what this psalm does. It is David's response to the Lord's love and goodness for answering his prayers. And nothing is going to get in the way of him thanking God and living it out loud. For us, sometimes things can get in the way of a thankful heart. We get sidetracked and distracted. When we begin to shift our focus off of God onto ourselves, we can develop a sense of entitlement. And we can't be thankful for something we feel entitled to. Everything we have is a direct result of the goodness of God.

WATCH THE DVD SEGMENT FOR SESSION 4, THEN USE THE FOLLOWING QUESTIONS AND DISCUSSION POINTS TO TRANSITION INTO THE STUDY.

- Do you ever catch yourself demanding something from God? Give an example.

- Pete talks about a "mindset of gratitude." What do you think that looks like in our everyday lives?

WHAT DOES THE BIBLE SAY?

ASK FOR A VOLUNTEER TO READ ALOUD PSALM 138:1-8.

Response: What's your initial reaction to these verses?

- What do you like about the text?

- What new application do you hope to receive about how to live out the hope you have in Christ?

TURN THE GROUP'S ATTENTION TO PSALM 138:1-3.

QUESTION 2: What are the benefits of outwardly expressing our gratitude to God?

This interpretation question asks members of the group to examine the text and discuss how the kind of posture exhibited in the text is beneficial.

> *Optional follow-up:* What prevents us from outwardly expressing our gratitude more often?

> *Optional activity:* Encourage group members to complete the activity "Gratitude in Action" on page 41 of the group member book. Ask for volunteers to share their responses

MOVE TO PSALM 138:4-6.

QUESTION 3: What are some things people in your stage of life feel entitled to?

Answers will vary. The intent is to prompt interaction with the biblical text and reveal attitudes and conclusions that prevent members from being grateful

> *Optional follow-up:* What are some possible reasons for those feelings of entitlement?

CONTINUE WITH PSALM 138:7-8.

QUESTION 4: When has someone protected you without your awareness at the time?

It's clear in the text that God was often protecting David even though David was unaware of God's actions at the time. This question asks for similar stories from the group. Be prepared to share about a time when you realized much later how God was at work around you without your understanding or awareness.

> *Optional follow-up:* When have you had the chance to protect or support someone else without his or her knowledge?

QUESTION 5: What can you point to as evidence that God has not abandoned you?

This calls for members to cite Scripture and life experience with their answers. Invite personal testimony

> *Optional follow-up:* How can we encourage and support one another when we feel abandoned?

Note: The following question does not appear in the group member book. Use it in your group discussion as time allows.

QUESTION 6: What steps can we take to increase our gratitude and thankfulness toward God?

This is an application question included so that the group can share their action steps. It promotes accountability and the need to act on biblical principles .

LIVE IT OUT

How can gratitude grounded in hope be part of your life this week? Guide group members to consider the following actions:

- **Record it.** Gratitude is a discipline. Once a day create a list that reads: "I am grateful for _____ today." See how this simple act shapes your mindset about God's provision.

- **Say it.** Let gratitude permeate your conversations by speaking about what you are grateful for, rather than whining about how you wish things had gone.

- **Share it.** Choose someone to love for Jesus' sake. Do something this week that clearly communicates your gratitude to God: a gift or act of service.

Challenge: We may not be ungrateful, but we can forget to be grateful. We get used to the things we've been given, and we begin to take them for granted. Make it a goal over the next week to identify at least one thing each day you are grateful for and find someone to tell what it is you are grateful for and why.

Pray: Ask for prayer requests and ask group members to pray for the different requests as intercessors. As the leader, close this time by asking the Lord to help each of you walk daily in the hope of Christ and let gratitude flow out of you.

The Point: When you fail, Jesus will restore you.

The Passage: John 18:15-18,25-27; 21:15-19

The Setting: After Jesus' arrest, several people confronted Peter about his relationship with Jesus. Peter denied even knowing Him. After Jesus' resurrection, Peter returned to his former work of fishing, but Jesus called Peter to follow Him and show His love by shepherding Jesus' followers.

QUESTION 1: What are different ways people respond to failure?

> ***Optional activity:*** Help group members experience failure by finding several trivia questions that represent a high degree of difficulty. Challenge participants to come up with the correct answers and then unpack their experiences with the following questions:
>
> - What emotions are you experiencing right now? Why?
>
> - What ideas or images come to mind when you hear the word *fail*?
>
> - How do you typically respond to failure in your own life?

Video Summary: This week Pete talks about how hope helps us respond to life's failures. In John 18:15-18 Peter is confronted about his relationship with Jesus. And he denies Jesus. In John 21:16-19 we see Peter restored. The story of Peter speaks strongly to the truth that even the most devoted followers of Christ falter and fail. But regardless of where we are or what we've done, Jesus is the restorer of hope. And to fully breath in this hope we have in Jesus takes a day-by-day, moment-by-moment dependence on Him.

WATCH THE DVD SEGMENT FOR SESSION 5, THEN USE THE FOLLOWING QUESTIONS AND DISCUSSION POINTS TO TRANSITION INTO THE STUDY.

- Pete talks about how there is nothing we can do to earn a relationship with the Father. Are there ever ways you catch yourself trying to earn favor with Him? Explain.

- Share with the group a time when having a moment-by-moment dependence on Him helped restore hope in your life.

WHAT DOES THE BIBLE SAY?

ASK FOR A VOLUNTEER TO READ ALOUD JOHN 18:15-18,25-27; 21:15-19.
Response: What's your initial reaction to these verses?

- What questions do you have about these verses?

- What new application do you hope to get from this passage?

TURN THE GROUP'S ATTENTION TO JOHN 18:15-18,25-27.
QUESTION 2: How do you respond to Peter's fear of being identified with Jesus?

We included this question because most of us—if we're totally honest—can relate to Peter's reaction. This provides group members with an opportunity to talk about their own fears and doubts in the context of Peter.

> ***Optional follow-up:*** When have you been tempted to act in a similar way?

QUESTION 3: How do we deal with the shame of repeated failure?

Jesus rejected the shame and accepted the pain. We often accept the shame and reject the pain. This question is asked to introduce the role of shame and how shame enters our hearts and lives through failure.

> *Optional follow-up:* What factors help us learn from our failures rather than become buried by them?

MOVE TO JOHN 21:15-19.

QUESTION 4: What is your emotional reaction to the events in this passage? Why?

Emotional reactions to specific texts are important because they connect us more intimately to the biblical events and people. This connection brings us closer to and helps us empathize with the biblical truths that are present in the passage. In this case, the restoration of Peter should open the door wide to a rediscovered hope.

> *Optional follow-up:* Encourage group members to complete the activity "Hope Sings" on page 51 of the group member book. Ask for volunteers to share their responses.

QUESTION 5: How can we help each other when we stumble or fail?

Group support and interdependency is a part of any successful group. This question is an opportunity to enhance both. It also provides an opportunity to apply our understanding of this Scripture to how we treat other people

Note: The following question does not appear in the group member book. Use it in your group discussion as time allows.

QUESTION 6: How would you summarize your experiences with failure and restoration?

Sharing and storytelling represent great ways for growing as a group. This question creates an environment for sharing relative to the text.

> *Optional follow-up:* To what degree have you allowed your failures to define you?

> *Optional follow-up:* In what ways can your future look different when you define yourself by your identity in Christ and the restoration He brings rather than the failures of your past?

LIVE IT OUT

Direct group members to these three actions they can take toward restoration and renewed hope:

- **Be honest.** Pray and ask the Holy Spirit to reveal your sins and failures. Turn from them and receive God's forgiveness.

- **Seek reconciliation.** If your sin has hurt other people, humbly ask for their forgiveness. Follow God's leadership to repair any damage you've caused.

- **Foster reconciliation in someone.** Listen as someone tells you about a failure. Pray together for God's restoration. Implement that restoration together.

Challenge: Failure is painful, but failure need not be fatal. With Christ, failures can lead to the beginning of something new. Spend some time this week reflecting on ways the Lord has used your failures to start something fresh in your life. Consider journaling about those things so you can revisit them any time you need a reminder.

Pray: Ask for prayer requests and ask group members to pray for the different requests as intercessors. As the leader, close this time by asking the Lord to restore each of you and replace your failures with hope.

The Point: After finding hope in Christ, we must share it with others.

The Passage: Acts 3:1-10

The Setting: When Peter and John were going to the temple to pray, they encountered a lame man who was begging. They did not give him what he asked for, but instead they healed him. This was the first public healing recorded in the Book of Acts.

QUESTION 1: What is something you had to share when you were growing up?

> *Optional activity:* Begin this discussion by leading group members in a spontaneous game of "Show and Tell." Ask for volunteers to display something they carried into the group meeting (including anything from their pockets, wallet, or purse), and to explain why that item is important and/or valuable to them. Conclude the activity by discussing these questions:
>
> - What have you found to be important and valuable in your relationship with Christ?
>
> - Are you satisfied with your current efforts to share that relationship with others? Explain.

Video Summary: This week Pete talks about the encounter Peter and John had with the lame man. The man asked them for money, but they healed him instead. Peter and John stopped to find out who this man was and what his real needs were. Then they offered him hope. The lame man received what he never dared hope for. The love of Jesus working through us sees other's need for hope. And a part of letting hope into our lives is sharing it. Truly sharing hope is sharing the hope we have in Jesus. When we show love, it points others to God.

WATCH THE DVD SEGMENT FOR SESSION 6, THEN USE THE FOLLOWING QUESTIONS AND DISCUSSION POINTS TO TRANSITION INTO THE STUDY.

- Peter and John had likely walked by this lame man many times before. Why do you think they decided to stop this time?

- Pete talks about how sharing hope involves opening our eyes and taking time to truly see people. What is one action you can take this week to live this out?

WHAT DOES THE BIBLE SAY?

ASK FOR A VOLUNTEER TO READ ALOUD ACTS 3:1-10.

Response: What's your initial reaction to these verses?

- What questions do you have about sharing hope with others?

- What new application do you hope to get from this passage?

TURN THE GROUP'S ATTENTION TO ACTS 3:1-4.

QUESTION 2: How can we discern the less obvious needs of others?

A discussion of discernment in this regard moves the group straight to the point of this session: After finding hope in Christ, we must share it with others. Sharing answers will help group members adopt a posture of discernment for others and their need of hope as well as a mindset for taking the time to really "see" people.

> *Optional follow-up:* How can we know when it's the right time to take action and meet a need?

Optional activity: Encourage group members to complete the activity "Sharing Hope" on page 61 of the group member book. Ask for volunteers to share their responses.

MOVE TO ACTS 3:5-8.

QUESTION 3: What obstacles or excuses keep us from serving people and offering hope?

This question asks specifically about obstacles to serving others. It is helpful to hear that others might run into the same problems. It also creates an opportunity to talk about how to overcome these obstacles as a group.

Optional follow-up: As a unique individual created by God, what can you offer the world and God's kingdom?

QUESTION 4: Peter and John healed in Jesus' name. How can we meet the needs of others so that it clearly points to God?

As we meet the needs of others, we want to take the opportunity to glorify the Lord. You might want to ask the group to look more closely at how Peter and John handled this situation and how that can be applied today.

CONTINUE WITH ACTS 3:9-10.

QUESTION 5: How have you witnessed the ripple effect of helping someone in a small way that impacted others in a big way?

Answers will vary. The objective is a greater awareness of the magnitude of even the smallest token of extending hope to someone.

Note: The following question does not appear in the group member book. Use it in your group discussion as time allows.

QUESTION 6: Who in your sphere of influence needs to hear the good news of Jesus' death and resurrection?

The objective of this question is for everyone in the group to leave with a name on their mind.

Optional follow-up: What steps will you take to share that news soon?

LIVE IT OUT

Direct group members to three ways to share hope with others:

- **Open your eyes.** Take time each day to pray a simple but powerful prayer: "God, make me aware of those around me who may not know You."

- **Open your home.** As you become aware of people who are not Christ followers, establish relationships with them. Let them see Jesus in you. Invite them over to share a meal.

- **Open your mouth.** Share your story of hope with a friend or coworker. How has Jesus brought you through a rough time?

Challenge: God gave you hope when He healed your past through Jesus Christ. You've got something worth sharing. This week look for opportunities to do just that. Don't be afraid to step out of your normal routine to share hope with a complete stranger. You may never know what kind of ripple effect you start with a little bit of hope.

Pray: As the leader, close this final session of *Let Hope In* in prayer. Ask the Lord to help each of you as you move forward to use the principles you have learned in this study to experience hope in your lives, to share your hope with others, and to allow that hope to transform you on a daily basis.

BIBLE STUDIES FOR LIFE™

WHERE THE BIBLE MEETS LIFE

Bible Studies for Life™ will help you know Christ, live in community, and impact the world around you. If you enjoyed this study, be sure and check out these forthcoming releases.* Six sessions each.

TITLE	RELEASE DATE
Let Hope In *by Pete Wilson*	December 2013
Productive: Finding Joy in What We Do *by Ronnie and Nick Floyd*	December 2013
Connected: Our Life in the Church *by Thom S. Rainer*	January 2014
Resilient Faith: Staying Faithful in the Midst of Suffering *by Mary Jo Sharp*	March 2014
Beyond Belief *by Freddy Cardoza*	March 2014
Overcome: Living Beyond Your Circumstances *by Alex Himaya*	June 2014
Storm Shelter: God's Embrace in the Psalms *by David Landrith*	September 2014
Ready: Ministering Life to Those in Crisis *by Chip Ingram*	September 2014

If your group meets regularly, you might consider Bible Studies for Life as an ongoing series. Available for your entire church—kids, students, and adults—it's a format that will be a more affordable option over time. And you can jump in anytime. For more information, visit **biblestudiesforlife.com**.

biblestudiesforlife.com/smallgroups
800.458.2772 | LifeWay Christian Stores

Title and release dates subject to change.
*This is not a complete list of releases. Additional titles will continue to be released every three months. Visit website for more information.